WHAT DO YOU SEE?

A Conversation in Pictures

By Barney Saltzberg
Photographs by Jamie Lee Curtis

She took photographs of things she loved and sent them to him.

He drew pictures on her photographs of things he saw and sent them back.

She saw this on the ground and imagined all kinds of things.

She took a picture and sent it to him.

He imagined this.

She saw a friendly seagull carrying the world on its shoulders.

He saw a friendly monster who had no worries at all.

She saw something very silly.

So did he.

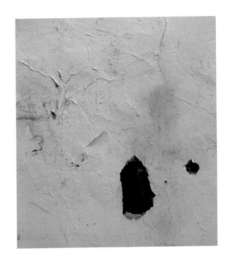

Sometimes she would see something.

And he would draw exactly what she had imagined.

She saw all kinds of things in this mess of noodles.

He saw a very hairy and noisy musical mess.

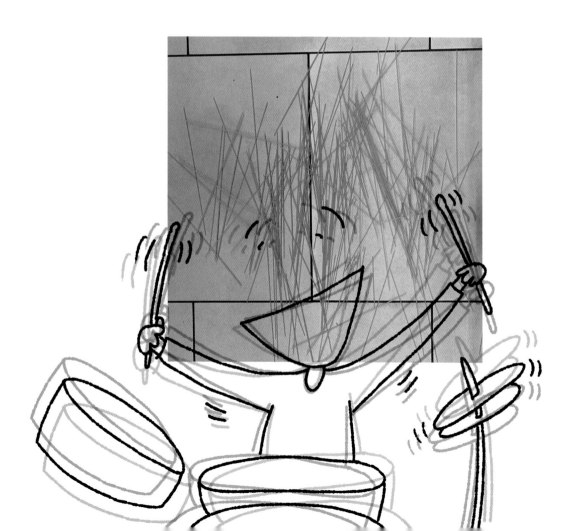

She thought this flower might turn into fairy wings.

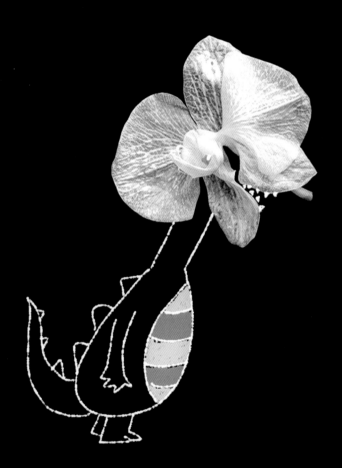

He had another idea.

They both saw...

Snails.

He loved what she saw.

A dog eating a fish?
A snail carrying a backpack?
An old person with a scarf?
Two large eyes?

She loved what he would draw.

They liked being able to see things differently.

How she saw. How he saw.

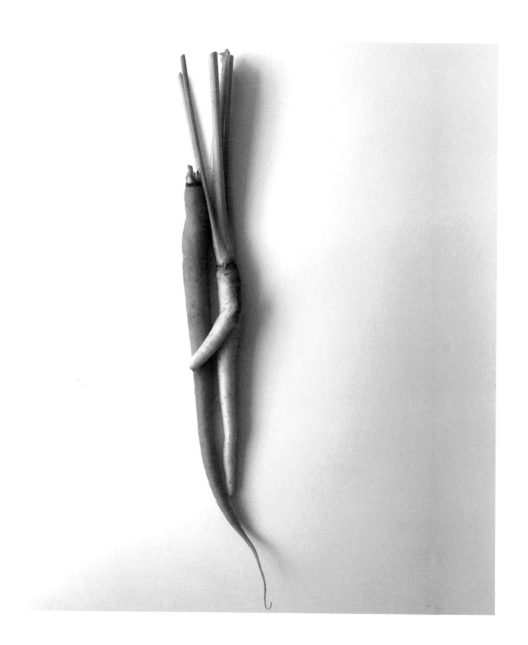

That's part of what made them friends.

How do *you* see things?

What can you see
in these pictures?

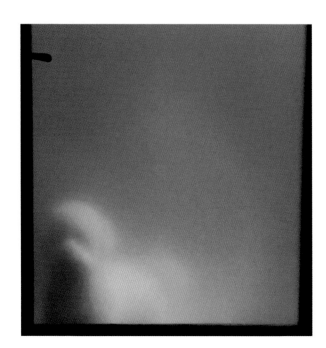

Activity Guide

Everywhere we look, we have the opportunity to look beyond what is there and see something new. In this book, the photographer shares her pictures and the illustrator uses his imagination to create something new. Here are some activities you can try at home to help you imagine and go beyond!

As you go through your day, look for patterns that you see in the world around you. You can find them everywhere — clouds, floor tiles, plants, even pillowcases! When you find a pattern, try to look at it in different ways so that you can find images inside or outside the pattern. Perhaps you see a furry monster inside of a spider plant or a lovable poodle as you stare at the clouds. Share your ideas with those around you!

Using an old magazine, tear out an image that appeals to you and use the image to create a new picture. Perhaps the jewelry ad turns into a necklace for an imaginary dinosaur!

Take a photo that you find interesting and see what kind of new picture you can make. Place the photo in the middle of a big piece of paper. Now draw the setting around the photo. Perhaps the picture of your family dog shows that he is actually on safari! Or you can draw right on the photo the way Barney Saltzberg did in these pages. What do you see that's different from how the photo first appeared?

For more fun creative thinking activities, check out Barney's YouTube Station, Createtubity!